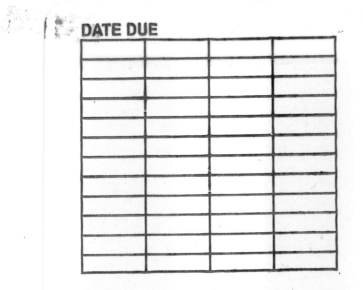

DATE DUE

COOKING
THE
HUNGARIAN
WAY

Lerner Publications Company
A division of Lerner Publishing Group
241 First Avenue North
Minneapolis, MN 55401 U.S.A.

Website address: www.lernerbooks.com

Library of Congress Cataloging-in-Publication Data

Hargittai, Magdolna.
    Cooking the Hungarian way / by Magdolna Hargittai—Rev. and expanded.
        p.   cm. — (Easy menu ethnic cookbooks)
    Includes bibliographical references and index.
    Summary: An overview of Hungarian cookery, including information about the country's geography, history, holidays, and festivals. Features simple recipes, menu planning, and information about low-fat cooking and vegetarian options.
    ISBN: 0–8225–4132–7 (lib. bdg. : alk. paper)
    1. Cookery, Hungarian—Juvenile literature. 2. Hungary—Social life and customs—Juvenile literature. [1. Cookery, Hungarian. 2. Hungary—Social life and customs.] I. Title. II. Series.
TX723.5.H8 H35 2003
641.59439—dc21   2001006612

Manufactured in the United States of America
1 2 3 4 5 6 – JR – 08 07 06 05 04 03

easy menu ethnic cookbooks

COOKING
THE
HUNGARIAN
WAY

revised and expanded

to include new low-fat

and vegetarian recipes

Magdolna Hargittai

Lerner Publications Company • Minneapolis

Contents

Introduction

What do you think of when someone mentions the country Hungary? Gypsies in colorful costumes singing love songs? Or composers like Franz Liszt and Béla Bartók, whose music is based on rhythmic folk tunes? Perhaps you have read about the Austro-Hungarian Empire, which played such an important role in European history during the 1800s and early 1900s. You probably think of Hungarian goulash, a savory soup seasoned with generous amounts of paprika.

All of these things are part of the heritage of Hungary, a small central European country with a long and dramatic history. Throughout Hungary's 1,100 years of existence, its people have endured many invasions by foreign powers and have lived under many kinds of governments. In good times and in bad, music and food have been important parts of Hungarian life. The music of Hungary's composers can be heard in concert halls all over the world, and Hungarian dishes like goulash, paprika chicken, and strudel are enjoyed by people everywhere.

Hearty goulash, with cuts of beef and delicious vegetables, makes a warm main dish to be enjoyed in the winter or anytime. (Recipe on page 42.)

The Land and the People

Hungary is one of the few countries in Europe that is surrounded by land on all sides. With nearly 36,000 square miles, it is close in size to the state of Indiana. It is bordered by Slovakia to the north, Ukraine to the northeast, and Romania to the east. Serbia and Croatia lie south of Hungary, and Slovenia and Austria border Hungary on the west. More than half of the country is farmland. Hungary's most important crops are wheat and corn, and its warm sunny summers create ideal conditions for large harvests of fruits and vegetables.

Hungary is divided into four regions. The largest region is the Great Plain. This region lies east of the Danube River, which flows through the center of Hungary from north to south, and south of the Mátra Mountains, which rise in northern Hungary. This plain contains some of Europe's best farmland, and Hungary's long river, the Tisza, flows through this region. Transdanubia lies to the west of the Danube River. This area of rolling hills and low mountains is home to Lake Balaton, Central Europe's largest lake, also known as the Hungarian Sea. Hungary's two smallest regions are located in the north. To the northwest is the Little Plain, which is mostly flat farmland. The rugged, heavily forested Northern Highlands in the northeast is the country's most mountainous region.

The capital city of Budapest is often called the Queen of the Danube because it lies on the banks of the famous Danube River. The cities of Buda and Pest united in 1873, blending their names to form

Modern machinery makes life easier for Hungarian farmers, who once tended their crops with horse-drawn equipment.

Budapest is home to nearly two million people.

Budapest. The part of the city that was once Buda lies on the Transdanubian side of the Danube and, like the rest of the region, is hilly. The area once called Pest is located on the Great Plain side of the river. This is where most of the inhabitants of Budapest live. One out of every five of Hungary's ten million people lives in the capital city. The national language is Hungarian or, as the natives call it, Magyar—a name that brings to mind the nomads who were the first Hungarians.

Hungarians have long been known for their love of music and their delight in flowers. And they are noted for their family loyalty and for their hospitality. In Hungary you may hear the phrase,

"Come as a guest, leave as a friend." Visitors are warmly welcomed and Hungarians willingly go out of their way to help strangers.

The History

In the A.D. 800s, a group of nomads called Magyars migrated from their home near the Ural Mountains westward to present-day Hungary. The Magyars settled in the grasslands along the Danube River where they found grazing land for their sheep and cattle. The Hungarian people trace their ancestry back to this group of nomads (traveling people) and still call themselves Magyars.

Hungary's first monarch, King Stephen I, or István, ruled from A.D. 997 until 1038. He was a strong leader who converted the Magyars to Christianity and united them under a central government. Much of King Stephen's work, however, was undone by the weak kings who followed him, making Hungary an easy target for the Mongols who invaded in the mid-1200s. The Mongols left when their leader died.

The reign of King Matthias Corvinus, between 1458 and 1490, was a high point in Hungarian history. King Matthias had a strong government backed by a powerful army. He made Hungary an important cultural center by sponsoring artists and scholars. This period was also an outstanding time in Hungarian culinary history. Traditional Hungarian ways of cooking were blended with western European techniques. Chefs were as important as wealthy landowners.

In 1526 the Turks took over much of Hungary. Their harsh rule lasted until the end of the 1600s, when they were defeated by the Habsburgs of Austria. The Habsburgs ruled Hungary with a heavy hand until an uprising, lasting from 1703 until 1711, forced them to allow the Hungarians more self-rule.

The mid-1800s was a time of revolution in many countries in Europe, and Hungary was no exception. Idealistic young people, led by the poet Sándor Petőfi (1823–1849) started a revolt on March

15, 1848. The liberal politician, Lajos Kossuth (1802–1894) became the first governor of Hungary. There was a fight for freedom, but the Habsburgs put down the revolt in 1849.

In 1867, after Austria had lost two wars, Hungary forced the weakened country to form the Dual Monarchy of Austria-Hungary. This arrangement made Austria and Hungary two equal countries with one ruler. Although this gave Hungary more control over its own affairs, many Hungarians still wanted complete independence. The economy was booming but millions of impoverished Hungarians sought refuge in emigration.

In 1914 the heir to the Austro-Hungarian throne was assassinated by a Serbian nationalist. Austria-Hungary declared war on Serbia, which led to the beginning of World War I (1914–1918). Shortly after Austria-Hungary's defeat at the end of the war, Hungary declared itself an independent republic. The country shrunk to its present-day size according to the terms of the peace treaty following World War I.

In World War II (1939–1945), Hungary became an ally of Nazi Germany when Adolf Hitler promised to restore some of the territory that Hungary had lost in World War I. But Hitler soon turned on his Hungarian allies and controlled the country until the Germans were defeated in 1945. Whole Hungarian armies and 600,000 Hungarian Jews perished in the war, which left the country in ruins. Hungary became a Communist country soon after the end of the war. Under the Communist regime, the arts and other cultural traditions were limited along with many freedoms and civil liberties.

In 1956 there was another revolution in Hungary, crushed by Soviet tanks. It was followed by yet another wave of emigration; about 200,000 people left the country within a few weeks.

The fall of the European Communist governments—including Hungary's—has brought many changes. Hungary became an independent republic again in 1989. Hungary joined the NATO alliance in 1999 and is expected to become a member of the European Union.

The Food

The Magyars and the Turks are the two groups that have had the most lasting impact on Hungarian cooking. The Magyars, the ancestors of the Hungarian people, were nomads who favored food that would travel well without spoiling. One common Magyar dish was *gulyás*, a soup made with dried cubes of meat that had been cooked with onions. This "instant" soup mix took up very little space and, when mixed with hot water, made a fast and filling meal. In modern times, gulyás, or goulash, is still a favorite Hungarian dish. Although the recipe has changed over the years—it is no longer dried and can include anything from green peppers to tomatoes—it owes its beginnings to the Magyars' simple soup.

Another Hungarian specialty that dates back to the Magyars is *tarhonya*, a pasta made of a flour and egg dough that has been crumbled

Outdoor markets are very popular for buying fresh fruits and vegetables in Budapest.

into pea-sized balls and dried. Because it could be stored indefinitely, this pasta was very convenient for the migrating life of the nomads.

The Magyars also introduced a cooking utensil called a *bogrács*. A bogrács is a copper or cast-iron kettle that is suspended from a sturdy stick over an open fire. Hungarians still use a bogrács on cookouts when making a dish such as goulash or fish stew. In many restaurants, these dishes are served in a mini-bogrács over a flame.

The most characteristic ingredient of Hungarian cooking is paprika, a spice made of ground dried red peppers. Paprika is believed to have come from the Americas. It first appeared in Hungary in the 1500s during the Turkish occupation. At first, paprika was used only

Children help make goulash in a bogrács, or kettle, hung over a fire.

by the lower classes. It was eventually discovered by the nobility and became an essential part of Hungarian cuisine by the middle of the 1800s. In 1937 Hungarian professor Albert Szent-Gyorgyi won the Nobel Prize for physiology and medicine when he discovered that paprika is the world's richest source of vitamin C.

Paprika can be quite hot, and many people have come to associate Hungary with very spicy food. But a typical Hungarian meal is not necessarily made with strong paprika. Powdered paprika comes in a great variety of strengths, from mild and slightly sweet to red hot. There is a paprika to please every taste.

Strudel and coffee are two Hungarian treats that were also introduced during the Turkish occupation. The Turks ate a delicious pastry made of paper-thin sheets of dough, called phyllo, that were baked with a filling of nuts and honey. The Hungarians took the phyllo dough and filled it with a variety of sweet fillings, such as cherries or poppy seeds, to make strudel. Coffee, a perfect accompaniment to strudel, was introduced to Hungary at the same time as phyllo dough. A small cup of very strong coffee with sugar and milk or cream, or even without, is an important part of a Hungarian meal.

Traditional Hungarian meals are often heavy and have given way, in modern times, to lighter fare. But even serious weight watchers give up their diets on holidays and during special get-togethers with friends and relatives. At the beginning of a meal, Hungarians wish each other "Good appetite." When they finish eating, diners thank their host or hostess. The traditional response is: "To your health!"

Holidays and Festivals

Hungarians, like other people, like to brighten their everyday lives with festivals and holidays. Many festivals originate in ancient Hungarian folklore and are celebrated all over the country. There are also smaller, local festivities that are connected to special events in a village or town.

August 20 is national holiday in Hungary honoring King Stephen (István). This first king, who became a saint, was the founder of the state of Hungary. In Budapest, Saint Stephen's Day is celebrated with live performances on and over the Danube River. The highlight of the day's festivities is a spectacular fireworks display. After the fireworks there are street balls with live music and dancing. Traffic halts for the occasion. St. Stephen's Day is also called the Day of the New Bread. Hungarians consider bread to be the basis of life, and the most important food. August is the month when the wheat harvest is brought in, and the first new flour of the year is used to bake new bread.

Hungarians celebrate two other national holidays. March 15 recalls the 1848 revolution against the Habsburgs, and October 23 recognizes the 1956 revolution against the Soviet Union.

Christmas and Easter are important family holidays. People plan and prepare for the festive holiday meals far in advance. Christmas specialties, whether pastries or cookies, are often given as gifts. Cooks serve these gifts along with their own creations at holiday get-togethers.

The traditional dish for Christmas Eve is fish, either fried or as a special fish soup, called *halászlé*, and some families have both. The fried fish is usually carp, and the soup is prepared from different types of fish with onions and a lot of paprika. The popular walnut roll and poppy seed roll are a must for dessert.

Christmas Day dinner is usually shared with family members or friends and the table is decorated as suited to the occasion. As with most formal Hungarian dinners, it starts with an appetizer and a soup course. Each family usually has its own traditional Christmas menu. Many have a rich chicken soup followed by roasted or fried pork, potatoes, rice, and vegetables. There are also different salads along with the main course. Other families prefer a beef soup, followed by roast turkey, with the same kinds of accompaniments. Christmas dinner is usually finished with a rich walnut- or chocolate-layered cake.

Dessert is an important part of Christmas. Each family prepares many different types, and they are arranged elegantly on large china dishes. It could be a selection of flaky strudels with different kinds of fillings, or rolled cakes filled with poppy seeds or walnuts. Chocolate is used in many desserts, either as filling or as topping. A layered cake, called *zserbó*, filled with walnuts and jam and covered by a thick layer of dark chocolate, is everybody's favorite.

New Year's Eve is another festive occasion all over the country. People start celebrating as early as late afternoon, walking in the streets with enormous paper trumpets, making a lot of noise. Some streets in Budapest are closed to traffic so people can crowd into them. Later, people continue the partying until dawn, at home or at the many restaurants or theaters in town.

On New Year's Day, many Hungarians promise to start a diet to lose weight. Lentil soup is a favorite New Year's meal. Lentils, small and round, look a bit like coins and are believed to bring luck and riches during the coming year.

Easter is an all-day celebration. Most families make or buy colorful eggs to decorate their home for the holiday. Easter Sunday starts with a brunch that includes a braided loaf made of sweet dough. The Easter ham is served on a big platter surrounded by eggs that were boiled in the liquid in which the ham was cooked to get a special flavor and color. Some colored eggs are also added to the platter. Freshly grated horseradish root, either by itself or made into a horseradish sauce, and strong mustard are a must to serve with the ham.

The holiday continues on Easter Monday. It features an old folk tradition called "sprinkling" or "watering" that is anxiously awaited by Hungarian youngsters. Traditionally, in the villages, boys went to the homes of young girls and dumped buckets of water over the girls' heads. The water was meant to have cleansing and fertilizing power. Boys, in turn, were supposed to get a gift from the girl they "sprinkled." Traditionally, this gift was a painted egg that the girl had made herself. In modern days, boys visit girls and sprinkle a little cologne or perfume on their heads. Girls then present boys with an egg or with chocolate eggs and store-bought Easter candies or other gifts. Popular girls take pride in having many boys sprinkle them on Easter Monday.

Hungarians also hold festivals built around local specialties. Kalocsa Paprika Day, for example, celebrates the red spice that is the national flavor. Kalocsa is a small town that is famous for its paprika. During September and October, the thousands of acres of flaming red pepper fields are ready for harvesting. Visitors coming for the two-week festival, which is held in mid-September, may help with the paprika harvest. They also taste typical Hungarian dishes prepared with lots of paprika, sometimes sweet but most often quite hot. Paprika Day always closes with Hungarian folk dances and shows. Visitors may also visit Kalocsa's paprika museum, the only one in Europe, to learn of paprika's long journey to Hungary from the Americas through Turkey.

Dancing, as well as food, is an important part of celebrations in Hungary. Here young dancers perform an old folkdance in the ancient costume of the region.

Fans of sausages flock to Békéscsaba in late October for the Sausage Festival of Csaba. The festival features the preparation of all sorts of meat products according to traditional methods. *Kolbász* is the name of the pork sausage for which Békéscsaba is famous. It is similar to the Polish kielbasa well known in the United States. Its main ingredients are different cuts of pork, paprika, salt, a little caraway seed, and garlic. The final touch is smoking. During the four-day festival, student butchers compete to see who can make different types of fresh sausage the best. At the same time, folk groups present music and dances. Just to keep things lively, there are also pickle-making contests and quizzes about folk traditions.

Just as the residents of Csaba compete to see who makes the best sausage, the fishermen of Baja compete to see who can cook up the best fish soup. The contest is the main event of the Fish Soup Festival in Baja, a city on the bank of the Danube River in southern Hungary. The soup, called *halászlé*, along with other fish dishes, is traditionally made by the man of the house. The soup festival takes place in the huge main square of the town, where cooks prepare the soup in large kettles. Lively folk music plays in the background, and festival-goers sample the local wine and dance. At the end of the day, judges taste the soups and the winning cook is announced. The festival ends with fireworks at midnight.

Before You Begin

Hungarian cooking makes use of some ingredients that you may not know. Sometimes special cookware is used, too, although the recipes in this book can easily be prepared with ordinary utensils and pans.

The most important thing you need to know before you start is how to be a careful cook. On the following page, you'll find a few rules that will make your cooking experience safe, fun, and easy. Next, take a look at the "dictionary" of utensils, terms, and special ingredients. You may also want to read the list of tips on preparing healthy, low-fat meals.

When you've picked out a recipe to try, read through it from beginning to end. Now you are ready to shop for ingredients and to organize the cookware you will need. Once you have assembled everything, you're ready to begin cooking. When preparing recipes that call for sautéing ingredients in oil, measure out the spices and herbs, wash any fresh vegetables, and do all of the cutting and chopping called for in the recipe before you heat up the oil. Then, once the oil is hot, you'll be able to add each ingredient quickly and easily.

Tomato salad makes a good appetizer or side dish for any meal. (Recipe on page 45.)

The Careful Cook

Whenever you cook, there are certain safety rules you must always keep in mind. Even experienced cooks follow these rules when they are in the kitchen.

- Always wash your hands before handling food. Thoroughly wash all raw vegetables and fruits to remove dirt, chemicals, and insecticides. Wash uncooked poultry, fish, and meat under cold water.
- Use a cutting board when cutting up vegetables and fruits. Don't cut them up in your hand! And be sure to cut in a direction *away* from you and your fingers.
- Long hair or loose clothing can easily catch fire if brought near the burners of a stove. If you have long hair, tie it back before you start cooking.
- Turn all pot handles toward the back of the stove so that you will not catch your sleeves or jewelry on them. This is especially important when younger brothers and sisters are around. They could easily knock off a pot and get burned.
- Always use a pot holder to steady hot pots or to take pans out of the oven. Don't use a wet cloth on a hot pan because the steam it produces could burn you.
- Lift the lid of a steaming pot with the opening away from you so that you will not get burned.
- If you get burned, hold the burn under cold running water. Do not put grease or butter on it. Cold water helps to take the heat out, but grease or butter will only keep it in.
- If grease or cooking oil catches fire, throw baking soda or salt at the bottom of the flame to put it out. (Water will *not* put out a grease fire.) Call for help, and try to turn all the stove burners to "off."

Cooking Utensils

colander—A bowl with holes in the bottom and sides. It is used for draining liquid from a solid food.

cruet—A slender, glass bottle with a tight-fitting top, used to prepare and store salad dressing

Dutch oven—A heavy pot with a tight-fitting domed lid that is often used for cooking soups or stews

pastry brush—A small brush with nylon bristles used for coating food with melted butter or other liquids

sieve—A bowl-shaped utensil made of mesh used to wash or drain small, fine foods

spatula—A flat, thin utensil, made of metal, plastic, or rubber, used to lift, toss, turn, or scoop up food

Cooking Terms

boil—To heat a liquid over high heat until bubbles form and rise rapidly to the surface

brown—To cook food quickly in fat over high heat so that the surface turns an even brown

core—To remove the center part of a fruit or vegetable that contains the stem and/or seed

cream—To beat several ingredients together until the mixture has a smooth consistency

fold—To blend an ingredient with other ingredients by using a gentle overturning circular motion instead of by stirring or beating

garnish—To decorate with small pieces of food such as sprigs of parsley

knead—To work dough by pressing it with the palms, pushing it outward, and then pressing it over on itself

pinch—A very small amount, usually what you can pick up between your thumb and forefinger

preheat—To heat an oven before using it

seed—To remove seeds from a food

simmer—To cook over low heat in liquid kept just below its boiling point. Bubbles may occasionally rise to the surface.

Special Ingredients

bay leaf—Dried leaf of the bay (also called laurel) tree. Remove leaf from food before serving.

caraway seeds—Aromatic seeds used in cooking

cinnamon—The inner bark of a tropical tree that is sold ground or cut and rolled into a short stick form. It adds a sweetish flavor to food.

cinnamon sugar—A mixture of cinnamon and powdered sugar. You can make your own by mixing one part cinnamon with three parts sugar.

cloves—A dark brown seasoning that is the dried flower of the clove tree. Cloves are quite strong, so use in small amounts.

dry mustard—A powder, made from the ground seeds of the mustard plant, that is used to flavor food

farina—A cereal made of finely-cut grain. You can use unflavored regular (not instant) cream of wheat when the recipe calls for farina.

paprika—A red seasoning made from the ground, dried pods of the capsicum pepper plant. It adds hot or sweet flavor to foods.

parsnip—The long, white, sweet-tasting root vegetable of the parsnip plant

peppercorns—The berries of an East Indian plant. Peppercorns are used both whole and ground to flavor food.

phyllo—Paper-thin sheets of pastry which can be wrapped around a sweet filling to make strudel or used as pastry cases for appetizers. Phyllo (or filo) is available frozen at most supermarkets.

pinto beans—Spotted, tan-colored, dry beans that are about the size and shape of kidney beans

poppy seeds—The seed of the poppy plant, mostly used in baking

Working with Phyllo

Phyllo dough is used with various fillings for Hungarian strudels and for a variety of other appetizers and desserts prepared all over the world. Phyllo is extremely fragile, but using it is not difficult if you follow these basic rules:

1. Thaw frozen phyllo in its original package for 24 hours in the refrigerator.

2. Do not unwrap phyllo until you are ready to use it. Make sure your work area is cleared, your melted butter and pastry brush are ready, and your filling is prepared.

3. Remove rings from your fingers and make sure your fingernails are not too long. (Fingernails can tear the phyllo.)

4. Work with one sheet at a time. Peel sheets carefully from package. After removing a sheet, cover remaining sheets tightly with either plastic wrap or a slightly damp kitchen towel (not terry cloth).

5. Leftover phyllo will stay fresh in the refrigerator for one week if covered well with plastic wrap.

Healthy and Low-Fat Cooking Tips

Many modern cooks are concerned about preparing healthy, low-fat meals. Fortunately, there are simple ways to reduce the fat content of most dishes. Here are a few general tips for adapting the recipes in this book. Throughout the book, you'll also find specific suggestions for individual recipes—and don't worry, they'll still taste delicious!

Beef and pork may be heavily marbled with fat. For recipes calling for meat, use a sharp knife to cut off excess fat. Also, in the past, cooks prepared 4 ounces (¼ lb.) of meat per serving. But 3 ounces per portion could be enough. If you want to be sure that the amount of food for each person is generous, increase the amount of vegetables instead of the meat.

Many recipes call for butter or oil to sauté onion, garlic, green pepper, and other ingredients. Using oil lowers saturated fat right away, but you can also reduce the amount of oil you use. Sprinkling a little salt on the vegetables brings out their natural juices, so less oil is needed. It's also a good idea to use a non-stick frying pan if you decide to use less oil than the recipe calls for. Using olive oil instead of other vegetable oils also makes the dish healthier.

Dairy products are a common source of unwanted fat. Sour cream is used often in Hungarian cooking. You can successfully use low-fat or fat-free sour cream in place of regular sour cream. The same goes for reduced fat versions of cream cheese and milk. When a recipe calls for cream or half-and-half, try using evaporated skim milk in its place.

Some cooks like to replace ground beef with ground turkey to lower fat. Buying extra-lean ground beef is also an easy way to reduce fat.

There are many ways to prepare meals that are good for you and still taste great. As you become a more experienced cook, try experimenting with recipes and substitutions to find the methods that work best for you.

METRIC CONVERSIONS

Cooks in the United States measure both liquid and solid ingredients using standard containers based on the 8-ounce cup and the tablespoon. These measurements are based on volume, while the metric system of measurement is based on both weight (for solids) and volume (for liquids). To convert from U.S. fluid tablespoons, ounces, quarts, and so forth to metric liters is a straightforward conversion, using the chart below. However, since solids have different weights—one cup of rice does not weigh the same as one cup of grated cheese, for example—many cooks who use the metric system have kitchen scales to weigh different ingredients. The chart below will give you a good starting point for basic conversions to the metric system.

MASS (weight)

1 ounce (oz.)	=	28.0 grams (g)
8 ounces	=	227.0 grams
1 pound (lb.) or 16 ounces	=	0.45 kilograms (kg)
2.2 pounds	=	1.0 kilogram

LIQUID VOLUME

1 teaspoon (tsp.)	=	5.0 milliliters (ml)
1 tablespoon (tbsp.)	=	15.0 milliliters
1 fluid ounce (oz.)	=	30.0 milliliters
1 cup (c.)	=	240 milliliters
1 pint (pt.)	=	480 milliliters
1 quart (qt.)	=	0.95 liters (l)
1 gallon (gal.)	=	3.80 liters

LENGTH

¼ inch (in.)	=	0.6 centimeters (cm)
½ inch	=	1.25 centimeters
1 inch	=	2.5 centimeters

TEMPERATURE

212°F	=	100°C (boiling point of water)
225°F	=	110°C
250°F	=	120°C
275°F	=	135°C
300°F	=	150°C
325°F	=	160°C
350°F	=	180°C
375°F	=	190°C
400°F	=	200°C

(To convert temperature in Fahrenheit to Celsius, subtract 32 and multiply by .56)

PAN SIZES

8-inch cake pan	= 20 x 4-centimeter cake pan
9-inch cake pan	= 23 x 3.5-centimeter cake pan
11 x 7-inch baking pan	= 28 x 18-centimeter baking pan
13 x 9-inch baking pan	= 32.5 x 23-centimeter baking pan
9 x 5-inch loaf pan	= 23 x 13-centimeter loaf pan
2-quart casserole	= 2-liter casserole

A Hungarian Table

In early times in small villages, Hungarians used to cover their tables with beautifully embroidered cloths. The patterns could be flowers or geometric designs. The embroidery was done by hand and the cloths were passed down through generations of a family. Embroidering is a type of Hungarian folk art, and different regions in the country have their own distinct and different patterns and colors. Bright greens, blues, reds, and yellows in different shades are popular colors. The ancient Hungarian folk dishware is colorful, too, and also varies from region to region.

Folk costumes, embroidered table cloths, and richly decorated dishware can still be bought in the many shops in tourist centers all over Hungary and are very popular among foreign visitors. However, they are no longer used by most Hungarians and have not been for a long time, except, perhaps, in some small villages.

Musicians serenade a family as they dine at a fancy Hungarian restaurant.

A Hungarian Menu

Below are menu plans for a typical Hungarian midday dinner and evening supper. The shopping lists of items you will need to prepare these meals are included. All the recipes are found in this book.

DINNER

Cold cherry soup

Paprika chicken with small dumplings

Tomato salad

Pancakes with walnut filling and chocolate sauce

SHOPPING LIST:

Produce

1 lemon
6 to 8 firm tomatoes
2 onions
1 green pepper
parsley

Dairy/Egg/Meat

1 2½–3 lb. chicken
4 eggs
butter or margarine
milk
1 pt. half-and-half
12 oz. sour cream
whipping cream

Canned/Bottled/Boxed

1 20-oz. can cherry pie
   filling
vegetable or salad oil
white vinegar
chocolate syrup
apricot jam
vanilla extract

Miscellaneous

cloves, whole
cinnamon, ground
cinnamon stick
flour
sugar
salt
paprika
finely chopped walnuts
raisins

SUPPER

Stuffed green peppers
with potatoes

Strudel with cottage
cheese filling

Fresh fruit in season

SHOPPING LIST:

Produce

6 large green peppers
12 small/medium-size
   potatoes
1 small onion
1 lemon
Fruit to serve six—apples,
   pears, apricots, plums, or
   cherries, depending on the
   season

Dairy/Egg/Meat

1 lb. lean ground beef,
   turkey, or pork
2 eggs
butter, unsalted
16 oz. small-curd cottage
   cheese
8 oz. cream cheese

Canned/Bottled/Boxed

vegetable oil
rice
2 15-oz. cans tomato sauce
farina/Cream of Wheat
   (unflavored, not instant)

Miscellaneous

salt
paprika
ground black pepper
flour
sugar
powdered sugar
frozen phyllo sheets
raisins

Breakfast/Reggeli

Some Hungarians like to eat a light breakfast of rolls with butter and jam or honey. Or, they might have dark, crusty rolls with sliced cheese and/or ham. Others, especially those who live in the country, prefer a more substantial morning meal of salami, ham or sausage, cheese, eggs (prepared in any of a variety of ways), fresh green pepper rings, tomato slices, and rolls and butter. Any breakfast, however, is usually accompanied by tea or strong coffee for the adults and milk or cocoa for the children.

The Hungarian cold plate (bottom) and paprika cheese spread (top) make excellent dishes at an informal breakfast gathering or at buffets any time of the day. (Recipes on pages 34 and 35.)

Hungarian Cold Plate/Hidegtál

In Hungary, cold plate is eaten at almost anytime of the day. It can be served at breakfast or supper or as an appetizer at a party or formal dinner. If you are in a hurry at breakfast time, set out a plate of peeled hard-cooked eggs and ham slices with slices of tomato and green pepper.

½ lb. smoked sausage

2 to 3 hard-cooked eggs*

2 medium red bell peppers

2 medium green bell peppers

4 medium tomatoes

1 medium cucumber

various cheeses

green onions

½ lb. salami, sliced

4 to 6 slices ham

pickles

radishes

parsley for garnish

1. Remove casing from sausage. Cut into ⅛-in. pieces.

2. Peel shells from hard-cooked eggs. Cut eggs in half lengthwise.

3. Remove seeds and stems from red and green peppers. Cut peppers into strips.

4. Slice tomatoes.

5. Peel and slice cucumber.

6. Slice cheeses into thin slices.

7. Peel green onions. Trim roots and tips.

8. Arrange all ingredients attractively on a large plate. Tuck sprigs of parsley here and there on the plate. Serve with rolls and butter.

Preparation time: 20 to 25 minutes
Serves 4 to 6

To hard-cook eggs, place them in a medium saucepan and cover with cold water. Place over medium heat until boiling, reduce heat, and simmer for 15 minutes. Drain water from saucepan and run cold water over eggs until they are cool.

Paprika Cheese Spread / Körözött

Hungarians are very fond of this paprika-flavored spread and like to have it for breakfast, or as a midday snack with crackers or slices of rye bread. They often have it for dinner with fresh bread and a large bowl of mixed salad. Each family has its own recipe. Some versions are made with cottage cheese only (this makes the spread lighter and healthier), while others are made with liptauer cheese, a sharp cheese made from sheep's milk.

1 12-oz. carton cottage cheese

1 8-oz. carton whipped cream cheese

¼ c. minced or grated onion

2 tbsp. regular sour cream

1 tbsp. paprika

2 tsp. caraway seeds

¼ tsp. dry mustard, or 1 tsp. plain mustard

1 clove garlic, minced or pressed (optional)

1 to 2 tbsp. minced fresh chives (optional)

1. Spoon the cottage cheese into a sieve. Place the sieve over a bowl with the same size rim. The liquid (called whey) will start to drip out of the cheese. Let the whey drain out while preparing all the other ingredients.

2. Stir together the cream cheese, onion, sour cream, paprika, caraway seeds, and mustard.

3. Using a wide spoon, press as much liquid as you can out of the cottage cheese.

4. Add cottage cheese to cream cheese mixture, mixing well.

5. Turn cheese spread into a bowl for serving. Cover bowl. Chill in the refrigerator for at least 1 hour so that the flavors blend. Sprinkle chives over cheese spread just before serving.

Preparation time: 20 minutes
Refrigeration time: 1 hour
Makes 1½ c. spread

Hungarian Scrambled Eggs / Tojásrántotta

Four strips of bacon or turkey bacon cut into small pieces can be substituted for the smoked sausage in these scrambled eggs.

8 eggs

½ tsp. salt

¼ lb. smoked sausage, cut into ¼-inch pieces*

1 medium onion, peeled and chopped

1 medium green pepper, seeded and cut into rings

½ tsp. paprika

1. In a medium bowl, beat eggs lightly. Stir in salt and set aside.

2. In a large frying pan, fry sausage over medium heat. Add onion and green pepper and cook, stirring, until onion is transparent.

3. Add egg mixture and cook, breaking up and stirring with a spoon, until eggs are set.

4. Sprinkle with paprika and serve hot.

Preparation time: 10 minutes
Cooking time: 10 minutes
Serves 4

*Smoked sausage can easily be left out of Hungarian scrambled eggs for a quick vegetarian meal. If you do not use the sausage, you will need to use 1 to 2 tbsp. of butter or oil for cooking the onion and green pepper.

Dinner / Ebéd

The main meal in Hungary—dinner—is usually eaten between noon and 2:00 P.M., according to typical central European custom. Most people eat at the cafeteria of their workplace or at a nearby restaurant. Students and teachers have their noon meal at school.

Informal dinners consist of soup and a main dish with salad, sometimes also a dessert. More elaborate formal dinners, which take place later in the day, start with an appetizer followed by soup, one or two main dishes with salad, and dessert.

Chicken and pork are the most popular meats. A hot vegetable, potatoes, rice, or dumplings often accompany the meat dish. A salad of greens or pickled vegetables always accompanies the main course. Excellent breads of all varieties are available from neighborhood bakeries.

Bean soup with smoked sausage is a warm, tasty Hungarian dinner. (Recipe on page 40.)

Bean Soup with Smoked Sausage/
Bableves Füstölt Kolbásszal

½ lb. dried pinto beans

I medium onion, chopped (about
   I c.)

2 medium carrots

2 medium parsnips

2 tbsp. vegetable oil

1½ tsp. paprika

I or 2 bay leaves

I tsp. salt

2 tbsp. flour

5 c. water

½ lb. smoked sausage, cut into
   ¼-inch pieces

1½ tsp. white vinegar

½ c. sour cream

1. In a colander, rinse beans well under cold water and let drain. Place beans in a medium saucepan, with enough water to cover. Bring beans to a boil and boil 2 minutes. Remove pan from heat, cover, and let stand 1 hour to soak beans.

2. Peel and chop onion. Peel carrots and parsnips and cut into thin 3-inch-long slices.

3. Drain beans in a colander.

4. In a kettle, heat oil over medium heat for 1 minute. Add onion and sauté until transparent. Add beans, paprika, bay leaves, salt, carrot, and parsnip to kettle, sprinkle with flour and stir well. Add water and stir. Cover and simmer over low heat for 30 to 45 minutes.

5. Add sausage. Cook 55 to 60 minutes more until beans are tender.

6. Just before serving, add vinegar and stir. Place 1 c. of hot soup in a small bowl, add sour cream, and stir until smooth. Add sour cream mixture to kettle and stir well. Serve hot.

Soaking time: 1 hour
Preparation time: 15 to 20 minutes
Cooking time: 1½ to 2 hours
Serves 4 to 6

Cold Cherry Soup/Hideg Meggyleves

This rather unusual soup is especially popular in the hot summer months. In Hungary it is served as a first course, but it would also make a good dessert.

1 20- to 21-oz. can cherry pie filling

1 c. water

20 whole cloves

1 cinnamon stick

2 tbsp. lemon juice

1 pint half-and-half, regular or fat-free

1. In a large saucepan, mix pie filling and water. Tie the whole cloves into a little piece of cheesecloth* so that they can easily be removed from soup after cooking.

2. Add cheesecloth-wrapped cloves, cinnamon stick, and lemon juice to pan and stir well.

3. Bring to a boil over medium-high heat. Cook 5 to 10 minutes, stirring occasionally, so that soup will absorb the flavor of the spices.

4. Remove bag of cloves and cinnamon stick from cherry mixture. Cool to room temperature.

5. Add half-and-half, stir until smooth, and refrigerate. Serve cold.

Preparation time: 10 to 15 minutes
Cooking time: 10 minutes
Serves 6

*Cheesecloth is a thin cotton cloth usually sold in the housewares section of a supermarket.

Goulash / Gulyásleves

Although many people think that goulash is a thick stew, the genuine Hungarian goulash is actually a substantial soup. It is best when made from different cuts of beef, such as chuck and rump. Sometimes it is made with both beef and pork. It is often served as a main dish followed by a non-meat second dish or a dessert.

2 lb. beef chuck or rump (or 1 lb. each)

3 tbsp. vegetable oil

½ c. finely chopped onion

1 tbsp. paprika

1 tsp. salt

1 tsp. caraway seeds

2 tbsp. tomato paste

1 c. beef broth

4 medium potatoes

8 c. (2 qts.) water

1 medium green pepper, seeded and cut into strips

pinched noodles (see recipe on page 43)

1. Cut meat into ½-inch cubes (meat is easier to cut if slightly frozen).

2. In a kettle or Dutch oven, heat oil over medium heat for 1 minute. Add onion and cook until transparent.

3. Add beef cubes, paprika, salt, and caraway seeds and cook for about 10 minutes, stirring frequently.

4. In a small bowl, stir tomato paste into ½ c. beef broth. Add to beef mixture and stir. Simmer for 30 minutes.

5. Peel potatoes and cut into bite-sized pieces.

6. Add potatoes, remaining beef broth, and 8 c. water to kettle. Bring to a boil and simmer for 15 minutes.

7. Return soup to a boil, add pepper strips and pinched noodles, and cook for 10 more minutes, until noodles are tender.

Preparation time: 30 minutes
Cooking time: 65 to 75 minutes
Serves 4 to 6

Pinched Noodles / *Csipetke*

½ c. flour

pinch of salt

I egg

I tsp. water (optional)

1. In a medium bowl, combine flour, salt, and egg.

2. Knead until flour is absorbed, forming a stiff dough. Add 1 tsp. water if necessary to get dough to form.

3. Flatten the dough between your palms until it is about ⅛-inch thick. Pinch off ½-inch pieces of dough and drop into boiling soup, broth, or water. Cook about 10 minutes or until tender.

Preparation time: 15 minutes
Cooking time: 10 minutes
Serves 4 to 6

Small Dumplings / Galuska

Noodles and dumplings are popular additions to Hungarian soups and stews. Since shaping the dumplings takes time, you might ask a friend or a member of your family for help.

2 tbsp. butter or margarine

1 egg

1 c. milk

2 tsp. salt

2 c. all-purpose flour

12 c. (3 quarts) water

1. In a medium bowl, beat 1 tbsp. of the butter until soft and smooth. Stir in egg, milk, and 1 tsp. of the salt. Add flour, a little at a time, stirring well after each addition, until mixture is the consistency of cookie dough. If dough is too stiff, add 1 to 2 tbsp. more milk or water.

2. In a kettle, bring 12 c. water and remaining 1 tsp. salt to a boil.

3. Dip a teaspoon in hot water. Scoop up very small pieces of dough (about ¼ tsp. each) and drop carefully into boiling water. Dip spoon in hot water again if dough starts to stick.

4. Boil dumplings 2 to 3 minutes, or until they rise to the surface. If some of the dumplings get done before you finish dropping the dough, scoop them out with a spoon and place in colander. Drain all dumplings in colander.

5. Melt remaining butter in a medium saucepan. Add dumplings and stir gently until well coated. Serve hot.

Preparation time: 20 to 25 minutes
Cooking time: 5 minutes
Serves 4

Hungarian Salad Dressing / Saláta Öntet

This is Hungary's most popular salad dressing. The following tomato and cucumber salads use variations of this dressing.

½ c. white vinegar

1 c. water

2 tbsp. vegetable or salad oil

1 tsp. salt

1 tsp. sugar

1. Pour all ingredients into a cruet or jar, close tightly, and shake well.

2. Pour over salad and refrigerate for 1 hour.

Preparation time: 5 minutes
Makes 1½ c. dressing

Tomato Salad / Paradicsomsaláta

6 to 8 firm, medium tomatoes

1 small onion, finely chopped

Hungarian salad dressing (see recipe above)

2 to 3 tbsp. finely chopped parsley

1. Remove stem and core from the tomatoes with a sharp knife. Cut tomatoes into slices and place in a large bowl. Add onion and mix well.

2. Pour dressing over tomatoes and refrigerate for 1 hour.

3. Sprinkle with parsley before serving.

Preparation time: 15 to 20 minutes
Refrigeration time: 1 hour
Serves 6 to 8

Cucumber Salad / Uborkasaláta

2 medium cucumbers, peeled

1 tsp. salt

2 cloves garlic, peeled and crushed

2 tbsp. sour cream

Hungarian salad dressing (see recipe page 45)

½ tsp. paprika

¼ tsp. pepper

1. Cut cucumbers into very thin slices and place in medium bowl. Add salt, mix well, and set aside for 30 minutes.

2. Add garlic and sour cream to Hungarian salad dressing in a cruet or jar. Cover tightly and shake well.

3. Drain cucumbers in a colander and press out remaining liquid with hands.

4. Return cucumbers to bowl, add dressing, and mix well. Refrigerate for 1 hour.

5. Sprinkle with paprika and pepper before serving.

Preparation time: 10 to 15 minutes
Waiting time: 1½ hours
Serves 4 to 5

Paprika Chicken / *Paprikás Csirke*

Serve paprika chicken with small dumplings (see recipe on page 44) or with noodles prepared according to package directions.

1 2½–3-lb. chicken, cut into
   8 pieces*

4 tbsp. vegetable oil

1 large onion, peeled and finely
   chopped

1 tsp. salt

1 tbsp. paprika

¾ c. water

1½ c. sour cream

1 tbsp. flour

1 green pepper, cored and cut into
   rings

*After handling raw chicken or other poultry, always remember to thoroughly wash your hands, utensils, and preparation area with soapy hot water. Also, when checking chicken for doneness, it's a good idea to cut it open gently to make sure that the meat is white (not pink) all the way through.

1. Wash chicken pieces in cool water and pat dry with paper towel.

2. In a kettle or Dutch oven, heat oil over medium heat for 1 minute. Add onion and cook until transparent. Add chicken pieces to Dutch oven and cook, turning often, until lightly browned on all sides.

3. Sprinkle salt and paprika on chicken and add ½ c. water. Cover and bring to a boil.

4. Reduce heat and simmer for about 30 minutes, or until chicken is tender. Add a small amount of water if necessary.

5. In a small bowl, combine 1 c. of the sour cream, flour, and ¼ c. water, and stir well. Pour mixture over chicken and stir. Simmer, uncovered, for 5 more minutes.

6. Place chicken in a deep serving dish. Spoon sour cream from pan over chicken. Garnish with green pepper rings and remaining sour cream.

Preparation time: 15 to 20 minutes
Cooking time: 45 minutes
Serves 4 to 6

Supper / Vacsora

Because the main meal in Hungary is eaten in the middle of the day, the evening meal is usually lighter. It may be served any time between 5:30 to 8:00 P.M., when the family is home from work and school. Supper is usually a one-course meal, although some desserts can always be added. Supper can be a soup, a vegetable dish, or a cold plate of a variety of meats, cheeses, and vegetables.

Újházi chicken soup (top) or stuffed green peppers with potatoes (bottom) make wonderful main dishes for supper meals. (Recipes on pages 52–53 and 54–55.)

Újházi Chicken Soup / Újházi Tyúkleves

Újházi chicken soup was named for the famous 19th-century Hungarian actor Ede Újházi, who liked to cook this rich soup for his friends.

1 3-lb. chicken*, cut into 8 pieces**

2 large carrots, peeled and cut lengthwise into quarters

2 medium parsnips, peeled and cut lengthwise into quarters

½ lb. brussels sprouts

1 medium green pepper, seeded and cut in half

1 stalk celery, cut in half

1 medium onion, peeled and quartered

1 to 2 cloves garlic, peeled

2 tsp. salt

10 peppercorns

½ tsp. caraway seeds

1. Wash chicken in cold water and place in large kettle or Dutch oven. Add carrots, parsnips, brussels sprouts, green pepper, celery, onion, garlic, salt, peppercorns, caraway seeds, tomato paste, paprika, and water.

2. Simmer over medium-low heat about 45 minutes, or until meat is almost tender, removing foam that forms on the surface of soup with a large spoon.

3. Add mushrooms and frozen sweet peas and cook 15 minutes longer, until meat is very tender.

4. Place a sieve over a large kettle. Carefully pour soup through the sieve. Set chicken and vegetables aside to cool. Do not discard the broth.

*Never thaw frozen chicken at room temperature. Leave it in the original wrapping and place in the refrigerator. To thaw more quickly, place the chicken, still wrapped, in cold water, changing the water every 30 minutes.

1 tbsp. tomato paste

½ tsp. paprika

8 c. (2 quarts) water

1½ c. (¼ lb.) sliced fresh
 mushrooms

1 c. frozen sweet peas

1 c. (4 oz.) very fine egg noodles
 such as angel hair or vermicelli

chopped parsley for garnish

5. As soon as chicken is cool enough
 to handle, remove chicken from
 bones and discard skin. Cut chicken
 and vegetables into bite-sized
 pieces.

6. Reheat broth over medium heat.
 Add noodles and cook about 5
 minutes, or until tender.

7. Add chicken and cooked vegetables
 and heat through. Sprinkle with
 chopped parsley before serving.

Preparation time: 35 to 40 minutes
Cooking time: 70 to 80 minutes
Serves 6

**Kitchen shears are a great help
in cutting up chicken and other meats
and in mincing parsley and other herbs.
Wash them well after use.

Stuffed Green Peppers with Potatoes/
Töltött Paprika Burgonyával

This dish is especially popular in the summer and autumn when freshly picked peppers are available. Hungarians use a yellow, somewhat smaller-size pepper for this dish than the common green pepper available in the United States, but the taste of the dish does not depend on the type of pepper used for preparing it. Stuffed green peppers are usually served with boiled potatoes, but some people may prefer cooked rice.

6 large green peppers*

1 tbsp. vegetable oil

¼ c. chopped onion

1 lb. lean ground beef, pork, or turkey

1½ c. cooked rice (½ c. raw, cooked according to package directions)

1 egg

1 tsp. salt

½ tsp. paprika

¼ tsp. ground black pepper

12 small/medium-size potatoes

Sauce:

2 15-oz. cans tomato sauce

2 cans water

2 tbsp. flour

2 tbsp. sugar

1. Wash green peppers, cut off and discard tops, and remove seeds.

2. In a small frying pan, heat oil for 1 minute over medium heat. Add onion and sauté until transparent.

3. In a large bowl, combine ground meat with rice, cooked onion, egg, salt, paprika, and pepper. Mix thoroughly.

4. Stuff the peppers with meat mixture.

5. In a kettle or Dutch oven combine all but 1 c. tomato sauce with 2 cans (30 oz.) of water. Stand the stuffed peppers upright in the sauce.

6. Cover and cook over medium-low heat 30 to 40 minutes, until meat stuffing is tender. Use a large spoon to stir the peppers in the pot during cooking to avoid sticking.

7. While peppers are cooking, wash and peel potatoes and cut into bite-sized pieces. Put potatoes into a

kettle, cover with water, and
simmer over medium heat until
tender, about 20 minutes. Drain and
keep potatoes warm.

8. Add flour and sugar to remaining
1 c. of tomato sauce, stir well, and
pour over stuffed peppers. Stir the
tomato sauce well and cook for
another 10 minutes. Serve with
boiled potatoes.

Preparation time: 30 minutes
Cooking time: 45 to 55 minutes
Serves 6

*Green peppers are sweet, not hot, and a
good source of vitamin A. Choose peppers that
are bright in color, have shiny skin, and are
heavy for their size. You can keep them in the
refrigerator—unwashed—for five days.

Creamed Spinach with Fried Rolls/
Spenótfőzelék Bundás Kenyérrel

1 9-oz. package frozen chopped spinach, thawed

1 tbsp. butter

2 cloves garlic, peeled and minced

2 tbsp. flour

½ tsp. salt

1½ c. milk

¼ tsp. black pepper

2 to 3 white dinner rolls

2 eggs

¼ c. vegetable oil

1. Place spinach in colander to drain.

2. Melt butter in medium saucepan. Add garlic and cook 1 or 2 minutes. Be careful not to brown it, since browning changes the flavor.

3. Stir flour and salt into butter mixture. Add 1 c. milk. Cook over medium heat, stirring constantly, until thick.

4. Squeeze as much liquid as possible out of spinach. Add spinach to milk sauce in pan and mix well. Add black pepper. Cover and cook over very low heat about 10 minutes while making fried rolls.

5. Cut rolls into ½-inch slices.

6. Pour remaining ½ c. milk into a bowl. Beat eggs slightly in another bowl.

7. In a medium frying pan, heat oil over medium heat for 1 minute.

8. Dip both sides of roll slices in milk (do not soak) and in eggs and carefully place in pan. Fry each side 3 to 5 minutes, or until it begins to turn brown. Serve immediately with creamed spinach.

Preparation time: 15 to 20 minutes
Cooking time: 15 to 30 minutes
Serves 4

Noodles with Cottage Cheese / Túrós Csusza

This dish is a favorite Hungarian pasta that is served most often after a filling soup, such as a fish soup, bean soup, or goulash. Some people like it sweet, without the bacon. To serve this pasta as a sweet dessert, omit bacon, mix drained noodles in 1 tbsp. butter instead of bacon fat, and sprinkle with 2 tbsp. powdered sugar.

8-oz. (about 2 c.) wide egg noodles

2 to 3 slices bacon

1 c. small-curd cottage cheese

1 c. sour cream

1. Cook noodles according to directions on package. When done, drain in a colander.

2. In a large saucepan, fry bacon until nearly crisp. Drain on paper towel, and save bacon fat. When bacon is cool enough to handle, break into small pieces.

3. Add noodles to bacon fat. Stir well and cover.

4. In a medium saucepan, heat cottage cheese and sour cream over medium heat, stirring constantly, until hot.

5. Add half of cottage cheese mixture to noodles and stir well. Place on a warm serving dish, cover with remaining cottage cheese mixture, and garnish with fried bacon pieces.

Preparation time: 5 minutes
Cooking time: 15 to 20 minutes
Serves 6

Holiday and Festival Food

The Hungarian love of music and hospitality go hand in hand. And there's no better reason for enjoying good music and good food than a holiday. Nor is there a happier conclusion to attending a local festival than gathering at someone's home for food, drink, and music.

Holiday meals in Hungary, as in most countries, follow family traditions. Whatever the occasion, whatever the tradition, the foods featured in this book make wonderful holiday dishes. Hungarian cold plate and paprika cheese spread are ideal for serving while guests and family gather. Then the chosen soup and main dish, salad, vegetable, and bread can be brought to the dining table. Though it is nice to go out to a restaurant for special occasions, many Hungarians believe that the very best eating place is at their own home.

Strudel is a sweet treat at holidays and special gatherings. (Recipe on page 62.)

Strudel/ *Rétes*

Strudel, a sweet and flaky culinary delight, is the most famous Hungarian dessert. People eat it anytime, but it is a favorite on special occasions during holidays and at weddings.

6 phyllo sheets (3 per roll), thawed*

6 tbsp. unsalted butter, melted

6 tbsp. powdered sugar, plus extra for sprinkling

1 recipe cottage cheese or cherry filling (see recipe on page 63)

*Be sure to read "Working with Phyllo" on page 25.

1. Preheat oven to 350°F. Butter a 9 × 13-inch pan. Place a slightly damp, clean kitchen towel (not terry cloth) on a working surface.

2. Place 1 phyllo sheet on towel. Use a pastry brush to brush with melted butter. Sprinkle with powdered sugar. Put the next sheet on top. Repeat brushing and sprinkling. Repeat with third sheet.

3. Place half of the filling on the bottom third of the top sheet, leaving about 1 inch on each side. Fold in the two sides and, starting at the bottom, carefully roll up the sheets. If the phyllo begins to stick, hold the bottom corners of the towel and lift to loosen the sheets.

4. Place roll seam-side down in buttered pan, and brush with melted butter. Make a second roll with remaining filling and add to pan. Bake for 30 minutes, or until golden brown.

5. When strudel is cool, cut into 1-inch slices, place on dessert plates, and sprinkle with powdered sugar.

Preparation time: 25 to 35 minutes
Baking time: 30 minutes
Makes 2 rolls (about 24 pieces)

Cottage Cheese Filling / *Túrós Rétes*

¼ c. raisins

½ c. warm water

1 egg, separated

4 tbsp. sugar

2 c. small-curd cottage cheese

8 oz. cream cheese, softened

1 tsp. grated lemon peel

4 tbsp. farina cereal

1. In a bowl, soak raisins in warm water for 10 minutes. Drain well.

2. Mix egg yolk with sugar until smooth. Add cottage cheese, cream cheese, raisins, lemon peel, and 2 tbsp. farina and mix well.

3. In a small bowl, beat egg white with a mixer or fork until it forms peaks. Fold into cottage cheese mixture.

4. Prepare strudels as directed on page 62. Before spreading filling on phyllo, sprinkle bottom third of sheets with 1 tbsp. farina.

Enough for 2 rolls

Cherry Filling / *Meggyes Rétes*

2 16-oz. cans unsweetened tart cherries

2 tbsp. fine bread crumbs

6 tbsp. sugar

2 tsp. cinnamon sugar (see recipe on page 24)

¼ c. almonds, finely chopped

1. Drain cherries thoroughly.

2. Prepare phyllo sheets according to steps 1 and 2 on page 62.

3. Sprinkle the bottom third of the phyllo with 1 tbsp. bread crumbs. Spread half of the cherries over bread crumbs, and top with half of the sugar, cinnamon sugar, and almonds.

4. Follow steps 3 through 5 on page 62 to finish strudels.

Enough for 2 rolls

Walnut-Filled Roll/Diós Beigli

In Hungary, this Christmas treat is made with a yeast dough. Popular fillings for the roll are walnuts, as suggested here, poppy seeds, or an apple-walnut mixture.

walnut filling (see recipe on page 69)

1 8-oz. container refrigerated quick crescent roll dough

1 egg yolk

2 tbsp. water

1 tbsp. powdered sugar

1. Prepare filling and set aside to cool. Preheat oven to 350°F.

2. Unroll dough on a floured surface such as a bread board. Press closed the little spaces (perforations for using it as crescents) in the dough to form an oblong sheet of dough.

3. Spread the walnut filling to within ½-inch of the edges of the dough. Starting from the longer side of the sheet, roll up dough. Pinch edges to seal. Place roll seam-side down on greased baking sheet.

4. Beat together egg yolk and water. Use a pastry brush to glaze roll with egg yolk mixture. Let stand at room temperature for 10 minutes.

5. Place in oven. After 15 minutes, place a sheet of foil lightly over roll to slow browning. Bake another 5 to 10 minutes.

6. Cool completely on a rack before slicing thinly. Sprinkle with powdered sugar before serving.

Preparation time: 25 to 35 minutes
Baking time: 20 to 25 minutes
Makes 1 roll

Pancakes with Walnut Filling and Chocolate Sauce/
Diós Palacsinta Csokoládé Öntettel

These thin, golden pancakes are much like French crepes. Hungarian cooks serve them both as appetizers and as desserts. The best-known version as an appetizer or first course is Hortobágyi palacsinta, which is filled with a meat mixture. They can also be filled with mushrooms or spinach, and folded or rolled. As dessert, they may be spread with a walnut mixture, cottage-cheese mixture, or with jam or preserves. Palacsinta can also be stacked high, each piece sprinkled generously with vanilla sugar, and then served cut in wedges.

walnut filling (see recipe on page 69)

2 c. milk*

3 eggs

1 tbsp. oil

1½ c. flour

vegetable oil for frying

chocolate sauce (see recipe on page 69)

1. Prepare walnut filling.

2. If you are using an egg beater, beat together milk, eggs, and oil. Then beat in flour a little at a time. If you are using a blender or a food processor, blend the batter on high speed for 1 minute. The batter should not be thicker than whipping cream. Let the batter rest at room temperature for 1 hour.

3. While batter rests, get out a 6- or 7-inch skillet. Place the bottle of vegetable oil beside the skillet, so that you can reach it easily while cooking the pancakes. Have a heat-proof plate ready to hold the pancakes.

4. Make the chocolate sauce while the batter is resting.

5. When the batter is ready, heat skillet over medium heat. Add a few drops of oil to skillet and tilt pan to coat it completely (or use a spatula to help

coat the pan). Stir the batter and quickly pour 2 to 3 tbsp. batter into the skillet. It is best to use a small ladle for this purpose. Immediately tilt the skillet so the batter makes an even layer. The pancake will start forming tiny bubbles in a few seconds.

6. After about 30 seconds, use a spatula to lift the edge of the pancake to make sure it is light brown underneath. Quickly turn the pancake over. Cook just a few seconds on second side.

7. Remove to heat-proof plate and keep warm. Cook remaining batter.

8. Spread about 2 tbsp. walnut mixture on one side of each pancake, and fold in quarters or roll up. Serve warm, topped with hot chocolate sauce.

Preparation time: 25 minutes, plus 1 hour waiting
Cooking time: 1 minute per pancake
Makes 16 to 18 pancakes

For lighter, thinner pancakes, substitute sparkling water for half of the milk.

Walnut Filling / Diótöltelék

1½ c. finely diced or chopped
walnuts

1 c. sugar

¼ c. whipping cream*

¼ c. raisins

pinch of cinnamon

2 drops of vanilla extract, or
½ tsp. vanilla sugar

2 tsp. grated lemon peel

1 tbsp. apricot jam

*Milk can be substituted for
cream to make the filling lighter.

1. Make sure that walnuts are finely diced or chopped. If they are not, grind them in a coffee grinder. To avoid walnuts sticking to the grinder, mix with the 1 c. sugar and grind together.

2. Mix sugar, cream, and walnuts in small saucepan. Cook until thickened.

3. Add raisins, cinnamon, vanilla, lemon peel, and jam, and mix well.

4. Spoon walnut mixture into a small bowl. Cover and let cool at room temperature.

Preparation time: 15 to 20 minutes
Cooking time: 10 minutes
Makes 1½ to 2 c. filling

Chocolate Sauce / Csokoládé Szosz

Chill any leftover sauce to serve later over ice cream or vanilla pudding.

¾ c. canned or bottled fat-free
chocolate syrup

2 tbsp. heavy whipping cream or fat-
free half-and-half

1. Stir syrup and cream together in small saucepan. Cook over low heat, stirring occasionally. Cook 10 to 15 minutes or until sauce thickens somewhat.

Preparation time: 5 minutes
Cooking time: 15 minutes
Makes 6 to 8 servings

Index

About the Author

Magdolna Hargittai is a research professor of chemistry at the Hungarian Academy of Sciences at Eötvös University in Budapest. She spent about seven years in the United States as a visiting scientist at different universities, together with her husband and children. She likes to cook and entertain friends and is also interested in the cultures and culinary arts of other nations. She is also interested in symmetry, on which she has written several books for children.

Photo Acknowledgments
The photographs in this book are reproduced courtesy of: © Carmen Redondo/ CORBIS, pp. 2–3; © Walter and Louiseann Pietrowicz/September 8th Stock, pp. 4 (both), 5(both), 6, 20, 32, 37, 38, 46, 49, 50, 56, 59, 60, 64, 68; © János Kalmár, pp. 9, 13, 14, 28; © Ecoscene/CORBIS, p. 10; © Barry Lewis/CORBIS, p. 19.

Cover photos: © Robert L. & Diane Wolfe, front top; © Walter and Louiseann Pietrowicz/September 8th Stock, front bottom, spine, and back.

The illustrations on pages 7, 21, 29, 33, 34, 36, 39, 41, 51, 52, 53, 55, 61, 62, and 67 and the map on page 8 are by Tim Seeley.